W9-BIB-717

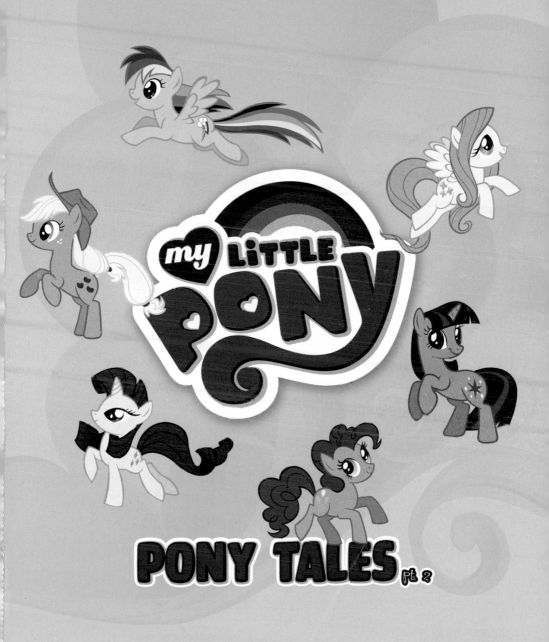

COVER BY **Tony Fleecs**

SERIES EDITS BY **Bobby Curnow**

COLLECTION EDITS BY **Justin Eisinger** AND **Alonzo Simon**

COLLECTION DESIGN BY **Neil Uyetake**

Special thanks to Erin Comella, Robert Fewkes, Joe Furfaro, Heather Hopkins, Pat Jarret, Ed Lane, Brian Lenard, Marissa Mansolillo, Donna Tobin, Michael Vogel, and Michael Kelly for their invaluable assistance.

ISBN: 978-1-63140-174-9   17 16 15 14   1 2 3 4

Ted Adams, CEO & Publisher
Greg Goldstein, President & COO
Robbie Robbins, EVP/Sr. Graphic Artist
Chris Ryall, Chief Creative Officer/Editor-in-Chief
Matthew Ruzicka, CPA, Chief Financial Officer
Alan Payne, VP of Sales
Dirk Wood, VP of Marketing
Lorelei Bunjes, VP of Digital Services
Jeff Webber, VP of Digital Publishing & Business Development

www.IDWPUBLISHING.com
IDW founded by Ted Adams, Alex Garner, Kris Oprisko, and Robbie Robbins

Facebook: **facebook.com/idwpublishing**
Twitter: **@idwpublishing**
YouTube: **youtube.com/idwpublishing**
Instagram: **instagram.com/idwpublishing**
deviantART: **idwpublishing.deviantart.com**
Pinterest: **pinterest.com/idwpublishing/idw-staff-faves**

Fluttershy

STORY BY
Barbara Randall Kesel

ART and COLORS BY
Tony Fleecs

LETTERS BY
Neil Uyetake

Pinkie Pie

STORY BY
Ted Anderson

ART and COLORS BY
Ben Bates

LETTERS BY
Neil Uyetake

Applejack

STORY BY
Bobby Curnow

ART and LYRICS BY
Brenda Hickey

COLORS BY
Heather Breckel

LETTERS BY
Neil Uyetake

Chapter One
FLUTTERSHY

ART BY *Amy Mebberson*

I WOULD BE SO MORTIFIED IF ANYPONY KNEW WHAT I'VE BEEN HIDING DOWNSTAIRS IN MY SECRET ROOM...

...OR EVEN THAT I HAVE A SECRET ROOM!

READY, ANGEL?

CLICK

CREEEEEK

JUST IMAGINE IF THEY KNEW THE TRUTH...

HERE IN MY STUDIO I'VE TURNED A SIMPLE CRAFT INTO A RADICAL ART AND CREATED OBJECTS D'ART THAT SCARE EVEN *ME*—

—EVEN THOUGH THEY WERE ALL MADE BY MY *OWN* HOOVES!

ART SOMETIMES TAKES CONTROL OF YOU, ANGEL! HERE I'M TRYING TO SHOW WHAT I THINK AND FEEL ON THE VERY INSIDE...

???

...BUT IT ALSO HAS ITS PRACTICAL SIDE!

LOOK! CHICKEN COZY CUPS—BOTH ARTFUL AND PRACTICAL. THIS'LL KEEP THEIR LITTLE EGGS TOASTY WARM!

OH, ANGEL, I WANT SO BADLY TO ENTER PRINCESS CELESTIA'S ART CONTEST...

BUT I'M AFRAID OF EVERYPONY'S REACTION TO MY ART.

THAT'S WHY I'VE ALWAYS KEPT MY CREATIONS HIDDEN AWAY DOWN HERE.

I HOPE PRINCESS CELESTIA WILL APPRECIATE THE SYMBOLISM INHERENT IN THE CHAOTIC JUXTAPOSITION OF MY CUTIE MARK MELDED INTO A TRANSFORMATIVE SPIRAL REPRESENTING THE PROCESS OF PERSONAL MATURATION AS EXPERIENCED BY AN INTROVERTED ARTISAN!

???

I MEAN THAT I HOPE SHE LIKES MY ART, BECAUSE IT'S ALL ABOUT ME LEARNING TO BE BRAVE.

SNIF! SOME PONIES JUST DON'T UNDERSTAND ART!

14

OHMIGOSH, ANGEL, THAT'S *PRAISER PAN*, THE INFAMOUS AND SAVAGELY CRUEL MODERN PONY ART CRITIC, AND HE'S *COMING THIS WAY!*

SNIF!

SOME PONIES THINK THAT A POT OF GLUE AND A PILE OF JUNK MAKES FOR ART!

CLEAN YOUR BARNYARD WITHOUT INFLICTING THE *REMAINS* ON US, WILL YOU?

SOME PONIES THINK THAT BEING ABLE TO SWAT PAINT ACROSS A CANVAS MAKES THEM AN ARTIST!

I HEAR THE SICKLY GRINDING OF *PINTO-PICASSO* TURNING IN HIS GRAVE!

SOME *OTHER* PONIES THINK THAT WE ADORE SEEING THEIR TRITE LITTLE *COLLECTIONS* ON DISPLAY!

THEY CONFUSE "ART" WITH "HOARDING."

SNIF! YES, *SOME* PONIES!

NONONONONO, IT'S NOT ME, NO.

FLUTTERSHY! IT *IS* YOU!

WHY ARE YOU HIDING UNDER THAT DREADFUL SHROUD?

YOU CANNOT WEAR THAT IN PUBLIC. I SIMPLY WILL NOT ALLOW IT!

BUT...

...BUT I DIDN'T WANT THEM TO KNOW THAT I WAS THE ARTIST...!

YOU?!

THIS EXTREME PIECE CAME FROM SOMEONE AS... INCONSEQUENTIAL...

...AS YOU?!

UNINTERESTING!

UNFASHIONABLE!

DULL!

OH, IGNORE THEM! I TOO KNOW WHAT IT IS LIKE TO SUFFER THE STINGS OF AN UNGRATEFUL AUDIENCE.

BUT YOU SHOULD BE PROUD OF YOUR CREATION!

PROUD!

OH, THIS IS WORSE THAN MY WORST NIGHTMARE!

PRINCESS CELESTIA!

GREETINGS, FLUTTERSHY! I LOVE WHAT YOU'VE CREATED!

YOU *DO?*

OH, RIGHT. I... UH... WAS DISTRACTED BEFORE.

I FAILED TO NOTICE THE SUBTLE METAPHORS INDICATED BY THE SWARMING TEXTILE ELEMENTS. ASTONISHING DEPTH!

SUBTLE.

ASTONISHING.

THEY'RE SAYING NICE THINGS!

THEY LIKE IT!

OF COURSE THEY DO—PRINCESS CELESTIA LIKES IT!

WELL, NOT EVERYPONY, BUT SOMEPONIES LIKE IT!

THERE ARE ALWAYS CRITICS, MY DEAR.

MEH.

A TRUE ARTIST MUST JUST CARRY ON!

24

ART BY Sabrina Alberghetti

Chapter Two
PINKIE PIE

ART BY Amy Mebberson

BLIP BLIP BLIP BLIP BLIP

WHOMP WHOMP WHOMP

WAS THERE AN *EARTHQUAKE* SCHEDULED FOR TODAY?

TWILIGHT!

TWILIGHT!

TWILIGHT!

WHOMP

HELLO, PINKIE.

OMIGOSH! TWILIGHT! I *WON*!

WON? WHAT DID YOU-U-U-U-U—

OKAY-SO-COLTA-COLA-WAS-HAVING-A-CONTEST-AND-YOU-HAD-TO-FIND-A-WINNING-CAP-AND-SO-I-DRANK-THREE-HUNDRED-AND-FOURTEEN-BOTTLES-OF-COLTA-COLA-AND-NONE-OF-THEM-WON-BUT-THE-THREE-HUNDRED-AND-FIFTEENTH-BOTTLE-HAD-A-WINNING-CAP-AND-I-WON-TWILIGHT!

I WON!

PINKIE, PLEASE, SLOW DOWN! ONE THING AT A *TIME*, OKAY? *WHAT* DID YOU WIN?

TICKETS, TWILIGHT!

HE'S PERFORMING *TONIGHT* AND I GOT *TICKETS!*

AND I WANT *YOU* TO COME WITH ME!

PINKIE. CALM DOWN. DEEP BREATHS.

TICKETS TO *WHAT? WHO* IS PERFORMING?

THE GREATEST CLOWN IN ALL OF EQUESTRIA

"PRETTY FUNNY"?! PONYACCI MADE *PRINCESS LUNA* LAUGH SO HARD SHE SPRAINED A *WING!*

HE GOT A *STANDING OVATION* FROM THE *GRIFFON KINGDOM!*

HE ONCE FOUGHT OFF A *RAMPAGING BEAR* WITH NOTHING BUT A *RUBBER CHICKEN!*

SOUNDS LIKE YOU REALLY *ADMIRE* THIS... PONYACCI.

YOU *BET,* MISTER! I'VE STUDIED *EVERY ONE* OF HIS ROUTINES! BOUGHT ALL OF HIS *JOKE BOOKS!*

I EVEN BOUGHT THE *TALKING PONYACCI DOLL!*

CLICK

"WAH-HEY-HEY! WHO'S READY TO *LAUGH?*"

ARE YOU HERE TO SEE *PONYACCI,* SIR?

NO, I... I'M AFRAID NOT EVEN *PONYACCI* COULD GET *ME* TO LAUGH.

WHAT DO YOU *MEAN*, SIR?

WHAT? OH NO NO NO NO! DON'T SAY THAT! *EVERYPONY* DESERVES TO *LAUGH!*

HERE— TAKE *MY* TICKET!

MAYBE PONYACCI REALLY *CAN* GET YOU TO LAUGH!

THAT'S VERY KIND OF YOU, MISS, BUT THERE'S NO NEED. I HAVE TO GO—ENJOY THE SHOW.

COME ON, PINKIE. THE SHOW'S ABOUT TO START.

FILLIES AND *GENTLECOLTS!* FOALS OF ALL AGES!

PREPARE YOURSELF FOR THE *ASTOUNDING ANTICS* OF EQUESTRIA'S *SILLIEST STAR...*

SO *THAT'S* WHAT YOU MEANT WHEN YOU SAID EVEN PONYACCI COULDN'T GET YOU TO LAUGH—

—YOU *ARE* PONYACCI!

THAT'S RIGHT, MISS.

BUT—BUT YOU WERE SO *SAD!* HOW COULD A *CLOWN* BE SO *SAD?*

WELL, THAT'S JUST IT, MISS—

—I'M SORRY, I DIDN'T ASK YOUR NAME.

PINKIE PIE! TWO P'S, TWO E'S, AND THREE *EYES.*

MISS PIE, I'VE BEEN A CLOWN FOR A *VERY* LONG TIME.

WHY, I WAS TREADING THE BOARDS BEFORE YOU WERE EVEN *BORN!*

TRAVELING FROM TOWN TO TOWN, PERFORMING NIGHT AFTER NIGHT...

I LOVE BEING A CLOWN— I LOVE MAKING PONIES *LAUGH*—

BUT EVEN FOR A *YOUNG* PONY, IT'S HARD WORK.

AND I HAVEN'T BEEN A *YOUNG* PONY IN A *VERY LONG TIME!*

ALL I WANT TO DO IN LIFE IS MAKE PONIES LAUGH.

COMEDY IS EVEN IN MY *CUTIE MARK!*

BUT BEING A CLOWN IS *DRAINING.* I CAN'T KEEP PERFORMING LIKE I USED TO.

SO I'VE DECIDED TO *RETIRE.*

WHAT?!

YOU'RE *QUITTING* CLOWNING?

I'M AFRAID I'M GETTING TOO *OLD* TO *CLOWN* LIKE IN THE OLD DAYS.

IN FACT, TONIGHT MAY HAVE BEEN MY *LAST PERFORMANCE EVER.*

"HEY, HOW DOES A BEE STYLE HIS HAIR?" "WITH A HONEYCOMB!"

CLICK

SIGH OH, PONYACCI DOLL. THANKS FOR TRYING TO CHEER ME UP.

PINKIE, I KNOW YOU'RE SAD BECAUSE PONYACCI'S RETIRING...

...BUT I'M TRYING TO GET MY GROCERY SHOPPING DONE, AND—

OH, DON'T WORRY ABOUT ME.

JUST PILE THE VEGETABLES RIGHT ON TOP OF ME.

I THINK TWILIGHT'S TRYING TO SAY THAT YOU'RE IN THE WAY, PINKIE.

OF COURSE I AM! WHY BOTHER?

WHAT'S THE POINT OF BEING IN A WORLD WITHOUT PONYACCI?

I THINK MAYBE YOU'RE OVERREACTING A LITTLE.

IT'S NOT LIKE PONYACCI IS GOING AWAY. HE'S JUST NOT PERFORMING ANYMORE.

THAT'S PRACTICALLY THE *SAME* THING!

A CLOWN WHO DOESN'T DO ANY *CLOWNING* IS HARDLY A *CLOWN* AT ALL!

HOW CAN HE JUST *GIVE UP* ON HIS PROFESSION?

WELL, LIKE HE SAID, HE'S GETTING *OLDER*. AND HE'S BEEN PERFORMING FOR A *LONG TIME*.

I DON'T THINK HE *WANTS* TO STOP, BUT HE CAN'T KEEP IT UP *FOREVER*.

BUT HE'S AN INSPIRATION TO *MILLIONS*!

HOW CAN HE ABANDON ALL HIS *LOYAL* FANS?

THIS ISN'T ABOUT *YOU*, PINKIE. OR ANY OF HIS FANS.

I'M SURE PONYACCI IS DOING THIS FOR HIS *OWN* REASONS.

WELL— YEAH, BUT—

IT JUST DOESN'T SEEM *FAIR*!

I KNOW IT DOESN'T.

BUT IT'S *HIS* DECISION, PINKIE.

I KNOW, I KNOW...

...I JUST WISH I COULD CONVINCE HIM TO KEEP *PERFORMING.*

I WISH I COULD'VE SEEN PONYACCI PERFORM. HE MUST'VE BEEN PRETTY *INSPIRING!*

SPIKE! THAT'S IT! YOU'RE A *GENIUS!*

I *KNOW* WHAT I CAN DO!

TWILIGHT! HOW MANY BOXES OF *GLITTER* DO YOU HAVE?

UH... *NONE?*

GREAT! I'LL NEED *ALL* OF THEM!

I'M SORRY, MISS PIE.

IF IT MAKES YOU FEEL ANY BETTER, YOUR PERFORMANCE WAS *EXCELLENT*.

FINE SINGING. GOOD JUGGLING.

YOUR *BALANCING* ACT COULD USE A LITTLE WORK, THOUGH.

HERE, LISTEN—

BOM BOM BOM

YOU SHOULD INFLATE IT A LITTLE MORE, GIVE YOURSELF A FIRMER SURFACE.

IS THAT A *Z&R* MODEL PARTY CANNON?

TRY USING *TWO* PARTS GLITTER TO *ONE* PART CONFETTI— YOU'LL GET A LARGER *BANG*.

THE MUSIC WAS ARRANGED WELL, THOUGH IF YOU HAD A *STRING* SECTION, THAT MIGHT BE EVEN *BETTER*.

DECENT LYRICS, EXCEPT FOR THE *OBLIQUE* RHYME AT THE END...

CEASE FIRE!

PONYACCI'S
SCHOOL OF
CLOWNING, JAPES,
AND **BUFFOONERY**

LET'S CHECK YOUR *PIE-THROWING,* RECRUITS!

CUSTARD! BULL'S-EYE! NICE JOB!

TROLLO LOLLO! WIDE TO THE RIGHT! TIGHTEN UP YOUR THROW!

I HAVE TO SAY, PONYACCI LOOKS *MUCH* HAPPIER.

AND HE'S GOT STUDENTS COMING FROM *ALL OVER* EQUESTRIA! THE SCHOOL'S A *HUGE* SUCCESS!

GIGGLE FIT! WATCH YOUR AIM! YOU ALMOST HIT *LAUGHING MATTER!*

WHY DIDN'T *YOU* ASK TO JOIN, PINKIE?

I'M SURE PONYACCI WOULD *LOVE* TO TEACH YOU.

OH... LET'S JUST SAY I'VE ALREADY LEARNED *PLENTY* FROM HIM.

"DEAR PRINCESS CELESTIA:

"TODAY I LEARNED THAT SOMETIMES IT CAN BE *HARD* DOING SOMETHING THAT YOU LOVE—ESPECIALLY IF YOU'VE BEEN DOING IT FOR A *LONG TIME!*

"BUT WITH THE HELP OF A NEW *OUTLOOK*, WE CAN *ALWAYS* FIND A WAY TO KEEP BEING INVOLVED.

"YOU'RE *NEVER* TOO OLD TO BE A PART OF WHAT YOU *LOVE!*

"I'M GLAD I WAS ABLE TO HELP PONYACCI KEEP BEING *FUNNY*—EVEN *OFF* THE STAGE.

"AND KNOWING THAT YOU'VE HELPED SOMEONE FULFILL *THEIR* DREAM...

"...CAN BE JUST AS GOOD AS FULFILLING YOUR *OWN!*"
—Pinkie Pie

END

ART BY **Sabrina Alberghetti**

Chapter Three
APPLEJACK

ART BY Amy Mebberson

SPLASH!

YOU SIMMER DOWN NOW, APPLEJACK! HAVING EVERYTHING JUST SO AIN'T WHAT THIS HOLIDAY IS ABOUT!

I KNOW, GRANNY—BUT THIS SEASON IS IMPORTANT TO THE FARM... AND THE FAMILY!

I COULDN'T BEAR MYSELF IF I KNEW I WASN'T DOIN' ALL I COULD!

AND WE ALL APPRECIATE IT, SIS! BUT YOU DON'T HAVE TO WORK ALL THE TIME, DO YA?

THAT'S RIGHT! TAKE SOME TIME TO ENJOY YERSELF.

EYUP!

DON'T Y'ALL WORRY ABOUT ME. I'M GONNA ENJOY MYSELF AS LONG AS MY FAMILY'S HAPPY. THIS IS GOING TO BE THE BEST HEARTH'S WARMING EVE *EVER!*

THE NEXT MORNING.

WHY, I COULD HAVE SLEPT TILL *NEXT* HEARTH'S WARMING EVE. BUT A FARMER'S WORK WAITS FOR NO PONY!

AIN'T THAT RIGHT, Y'ALL?

Y'ALL?

LOOK

LOOK

APPLE FRITTERS

APPLE FRITTERS

APPLE FRITTERS

APPLE FRITTERS

APPLEJACK! LOOK! IT'S *TERRIBLE!*

LOTS OF THE APPLES HAVE BEEN *STOLEN...*

...AND REPLACED WITH *SQUASHES!*

WHAT IN *TARNATION?!* HOW COULD THIS HAPPEN? WHO COULDA DONE SUCH A THING?

AIN'T IT OBVIOUS?

IT'S THE *SASS SQUASH!*

SASS WHAAA?

C'MON YOUNG 'UNS! I'LL TELL YOU AAALL ABOUT IT.

WAAAY BACK WHEN WE WERE FIRST GETTING THIS FARM OFF THE GROUND, IT SEEMED LIKE THE WORK WOULD NEVER END! WE HAD TO RAISE THE BARN, PLANT THE ORCHARD, DIG THE WELL...

...DAWN TO DUSK, IT WAS WORK, WORK, POLKA, AND WORK!

ALL SO WE COULD HAVE THE FINEST APPLE ORCHARD IN EQUESTRIA!

"YOU COULD IMAGINE OUR SURPRISE WHEN WE AWOKE ONE DAY TO FIND DOZENS OF TREES' APPLES WERE REPLACED WITH *SQUASHES!*

"WHO, OR *WHAT*, WAS BEHIND THIS MYSTERIOUS HAPPENING?

"WELL, HONK MY NOSE AND SHINE MY HOOF, I WAS GOING TO FIND OUT!"

57

"I STAKED OUT THE AREA FOR WEEKS! I HAD DONE NEAR GIVEN UP HOPE, TILL ONE DAY..."

Rustle   Rustle

"THAT'S WHEN I SAW IT! NEVER IN ALL MY YEARS THEN OR SINCE HAD I SEEN ANYTHING LIKE IT!"

WHAT WAS IT, GRANNY?

I DON'T NEED TO TELL YOU, I CAN SHOW YOU!

LUCKILY, I HAD MY CAMERA AT THE TIME!

YOU CAN'T TELL FROM THE PHOTO, BUT IT WAS DANCING, RIGHT THERE IN FRONT OF ME!

AND NOT JUST A NORMAL DANCE, HEAVENS NO!

IT WAS A SASSY DANCE!

I MUSTA SPOOKED IT, 'CUZ WE NEVER DID SEE IT, NOR ITS SQUASHES, EVER AGAIN.

TILL NOW, THAT IS!

SLAM!

WELL, IT'S NOT GONNA CAUSE ANY MORE MISCHIEF THIS HOLIDAY!

I'M GONNA CATCH IT!

WHEW! THAT'S THE LAST ONE!

ALL THESE MIRRORS BOUNCE BACK HERE.

IF THAT OVER-RIPE VEGETABLE COMES ANYWHERE *NEAR* THE ORCHARD, I'M SURE TO SEE IT!

AH!

BIG MCINTOSH! STOP CHECKIN' YOURSELF OUT! THESE ARE STRICTLY NON-VANITY MIRRORS!

LET ME GUESS, YOU WANT TO HELP? USING YOUR NET?

EEYUP AND EEYUP.

IF I SAID IT ONCE, I SAID IT AGAIN: I'M GONNA BAG THIS MONSTER ON MY LONESOME.

I APPRECIATE THE CONCERN, BUT YOU AND THE FAMILY SHOULD BE BUSY MAKING SURE EVERYTHING IS READY FOR THE HOLIDAY.

I CAN DO THIS BY MYSELF, AND I'M ABOUT TO PROVE IT.

DOUBLE DANG BLAST IT...!

MIRRORS ALL GONE.

I CAN SEE THAT!

...AND THAT'S WHERE THE PHRASE "NEVER TRUST AN ONION" COMES FROM!

UM.. EXCUSE ME, Y'ALL.

I'M SORRY, I... I COULDN'T CAPTURE THE SASS SQUASH. IT'S JUST TOO DANG ELUSIVE.

I... I'VE FAILED YA.

NOW, NOW APPLEJACK. DON'T BE HARD ON YOURSELF. THAT SQUASH HAS ELUDED CAPTURE FOR GENERATIONS.

I KNOW. IT'S JUST... I WANTED TO CATCH IT SO Y'ALL COULD ENJOY THE HOLIDAYS IN PEACE.

NONE OF THAT'S IMPORTANT NOW, DEARIE. WHAT'S IMPORTANT IS THAT WE'RE A FAMILY, AND WE'RE TOGETHER.

HEARTH'S WARMING EVE IS TOMORROW. WHO KNOWS WHAT IT WILL DO TO OUR REMAINING SUPPLIES OVERNIGHT?

YOU'RE ABSOLUTELY RIGHT, GRANNY! I'VE BEEN GOIN' ABOUT THIS ALL PIG-HEADED. THIS HOLIDAY'S NOT ABOUT DOIN' THINGS BY YOURSELF!

IT'S ABOUT COMIN' TOGETHER, AND WORKING WITH THOSE YOU LOVE MOST!

OH BOY! THIS'LL BE FUN!

AND BY GOLLY, THAT'S JUST WHAT WE'LL DO! WE'LL WORK TOGETHER AND CATCH THIS CRITTER!

69

SHUCKS, YOU'RE RIGHT, GRANNY. I *DID* GET A LITTLE CARRIED AWAY.

LUCKILY, I'VE GOT Y'ALL TO KEEP ME ON TRACK.

THAT'S RIGHT! 'CUZ WE'RE A FAMILY!

EEEEYUP!

DARN TOOTIN'!

"DEAR PRINCESS CELESTIA,

"IF THERE'S ONE THING I'VE LEARNED THIS HEARTH'S WARMING EVE, IT'S THAT HOLIDAYS CAN GET A MIGHT CRAZY. SEEMS LIKE THERE'S ALWAYS A MILLION THINGS TO DO, AND SO LITTLE TIME TO DO IT!

APPLE Pies

APPLE FRITTERS

Apple Pies

APPLE FRITTERS

"BUT IF YOU DON'T TAKE A MOMENT TO SLOW DOWN—REALLY SLOW DOWN—AND SPEND A LITTLE TIME WITH YOUR FAMILY, YOU MIGHT MISS WHAT THE HOLIDAY IS TRULY ALL ABOUT...

"...COMIN' TOGETHER, AND APPRECIATING JUST HOW IMPORTANT EVERY SINGLE PONY IS. AFTER ALL, EVEN THOSE CLOSEST TO YOU..."

Z

IT COULDN'T BE...

73

ART BY **Sabrina Alberghetti**

MY LITTLE PONY

MORE PONY ADVENTURES!

Get to your nearest retailer
and pick up these books
to add to your stable of
My Little Pony stories!

My Little Pony: Friendship Is Magic, Pt. 1
ISBN: 978-1-61377-605-6

My Little Pony: The Magic Begins
ISBN: 978-1-61377-754-1

MY LITTLE PONY
FriendShip is Magic

MY LITTLE PONY
The Magic Begins

www.idwpublishing.com